Mom
Tell Me One More Story

Created by
Kathleen Barber Lashier
and
Joanne Barber Farrell

Copyright 2003, ShoeStrings

ShoeStrings

P.O. Box 31
Pelican Lake, WI 54463
1-800-554-1345
Fax 715-487-5529
www.mymemoryjournals.com

Memory Journals for Special People

Grandma, Tell Me Your Memories .... Copyright 1992
Grandpa, Tell Me Your Memories .... Copyright 1992
Mom, Share Your Life With Me .... Copyright 1993
Dad, Share Your Life With Me .... Copyright 1993
To the Best of My Recollection .... Copyright 1996
To My Dear Friend .... Copyright 1996
My Days... My Pictures .... Copyright 1995
My Days... My Writings .... Copyright 1995
My Life... My Thoughts .... Copyright 1995
Sisters .... Copyright 1998
Heirloom Edition –
    Grandma, Tell Me Your Memories .... Copyright 1997
Heirloom Edition –
    Mom, Share Your Life With Me .... Copyright 1997
Heirloom Edition –
    To the Best of My Recollection .... Copyright 1997
Tassels and Tomorrows .... Copyright 1999
College Memories 101 .... Copyright 1999
From This Day Forward .... Copyright 1999
Mom, Tell Me One More Story .... Copyright 2003
Dad, Tell Me One More Story .... Copyright 2003

Printed in the United States of America
by G&R Publishing Co.
Distributed By:

507 Industrial Street
Waverly, IA 50677
ISBN 1-56383-150-3
Item #6101

About the Authors

Joanne and Kathy are sisters, and also mothers of grown children. In creating this book, they have drawn upon their memories of growing up in the same family, as well as upon the experience they share with you — the joys and challenges of raising children.

Joanne and Kathy's childhood memories center around their early years in Iowa. They are both former elementary teachers, and have previously collaborated on four Memory Journals.

Joanne and her husband Dave have two grown sons, Mark and Greg, and now live in northern Wisconsin.

Kathy and her husband Jack, also the parents of two grown sons, Andrew and Jackson, have remained in Iowa.

Every summer "at the lake" in Wisconsin, the growing family continues to create precious memories, mostly involving food, campfires, games, water sports, stargazing, storytelling and laughter.

*This book is dedicated to our parents
who taught us to be parents...*

...and to our children
who taught us to be children.

A Note From the Creators of this Book to the Real Author — Mom

You are about to share the story of the childhood of your son or daughter as you experienced it. This book will be filled with events your child was too young to remember, information she never knew, stories you never told him and your impressions when looking back on it all. You will be creating a treasured keepsake that will enable your child to see those times through your eyes.

The questions have been written as a guide to jog your memory. If you find that some do not apply to your family or you do not remember the information, we hope you will use that space to share photographs, clippings or other stories.

If there is not enough space to complete a particular memory, you will find extra pages at the back of the book.

May you enjoy the memories relived and may your child gain insight into what motherhood has meant to you.

TO: _____

FROM: _____

Place photo of you and your child here.

Table of Contents

Before I Was Born
What Did You Ever Do Without Me?

Tell me how you met my dad and what first attracted you to him.

You were married at

_____

_____

on the _____ *day of*

_____

at _____ *a.m./p.m.*

Did you go on a honeymoon?

Tell me about your job then.

What places did you live before I was born?

4

Before I came along to provide your entertainment, what did you like to do?

***Tell Me One More Story** about your life together before I was born.*

Get Ready
I'm On the Way!

How did you learn that I was on the way?

How did you tell Dad?

How did you tell others?

9

Describe how you felt while you were pregnant.

What did you do to get ready for me?

11

What are your BEST memories
of pregnancy?

12

What are your WORST memories of pregnancy?

Tell Me One More Story *from that time of our lives.*

Finally, the Big Day
My Birth Day

On the day of my arrival, what did you do at home before leaving for the hospital?

And then I arrived at

_____ *a.m./p.m.*

on a _____ ,

the _____ *of*

_____

in the year _____

at _____ .

Present when I was born were . . .

Describe my birth.

Tell about our first moments together.

On that day did anything make you laugh?

What frightened you?

19

What did I look like when you first saw me?

How did you choose my name and what other names did you consider for me?

What is your favorite memory of the hospital stay?

What is your least favorite memory?

Tell Me One More Story about that special day.

24

Home Sweet Home
Your Life Will Never Be the Same

My first address was _____

_____

_____

_____

Who was waiting at home for us?

I was lots of work. Did you have any help with me?

What was the hardest adjustment to make?

What did you rejoice over?

Were there any tears besides mine?

*Do you remember the first songs or
rhymes you sang to me?*

Tell Me One More Story *about our homecoming.*

All in the Family
My Relatives

Where and when were my brothers and sisters born?

My paternal grandparents are _____

_____

_____

_____

_____

When and where were they born?

*My maternal grandparents are*_____

_____

_____

_____

_____

_____

When and where were they born?

*Tell about my aunts, uncles, cousins,
and other important family members.*

How and when did my family come to this country?

__Tell Me One More Story__ about my family history.

Yummy in My Tummy
The Food I Ate

Was I breastfed? _____
For how long? _____

Describe the preparation of my baby formula and other baby foods.

When I was a baby, I loved to eat...

and didn't like to eat...

When I got a little older and learned to feed myself,
I loved to eat...

and didn't like to eat...

During my childhood and youth, how did you try to teach me about healthy eating?

What are your best memories
of mealtimes?

What are your worst memories
of mealtimes?

What were my early attempts at food preparation?

What were my favorite places to eat out?

What restaurant memories do you have of me?

Can I Have a Drink of Water?

Getting Me to Bed

Tell about my sleeping habits. Did I let you get any sleep when I was a baby . . .

. . . and when I was a little older?

What are your favorite memories about getting me to bed?

But sometimes I didn't want to go to bed. Tell me about that.

Did I have any special blankets, pajamas or cuddly friends?

When and how did I outgrow my thumb or pacifier?

Tell Me One More Story *about bedtimes.*

Diapers to Potty Chairs
I'm Growing Up!

What kind of diapers did I wear and who usually changed them?

When you got tired of changing diapers, how did you help me learn to outgrow them?

What words did I use for body parts and functions, and how did we arrive at them?

***Tell Me One More Story** about toilet training.*

Knees to Wheels
I Get Around

How and when did I first learn to move about, and what crawling adventures did I have?

What do you remember about my first steps?

Then I got my first wheels! Tell me about them.

Who taught me to ride a bike? Any
stories to tell?

What do you remember most about my learning to drive a car?

I know I was pretty excited the first time I had the car to myself. What was it like for <u>you</u> when I drove away alone?

Tell Me One More Story about my *knees-to-wheels adventures.*

Oowies, Illnesses and Other Disasters

It's a Wonder I'm Still Alive!

My memorable oowies include...

My memorable illnesses include...

What did you do to make me feel better when I was sick?

Was I ever "helpful" to you when YOU were sick or hurt?

Tell Me One More Story *about a time when I was sick or hurt.*

Are We Almost There?
My Early Travels

Where did I travel when I was young?
Tell me about my early trips.

What did you do to help me get ready?

How were car safety practices for children different then?

How did we spend long hours in the car?

What states/countries did I visit as a child?

What is your best vacation memory of me?

What is your worst vacation memory of me?

Which family vacation was the most fun for you?

If you and I could go somewhere together now, describe where we would go and what we would do.

Tell Me One More Story about our family travels.

You're It!
Games, Toys
and Pastimes

What did people do to entertain me when I was a baby?

As a child, my favorite games were...

What were your favorite and least favorite games we played together?

What did I do when I lost?

Did I make up any games?

83

When I was alone indoors, I used to amuse myself for hours by...

When I was outdoors, I liked to...

What special toys did I like when I was a baby...

...and when I was a little older?

Was there a toy I begged for but never got? Why?

Tell Me One More Story about my
playtime.

The Kid's a Genius!
Wisdom and Imagination

Tell about times I impressed you with how smart I was.

*What did I like to build, draw, invent,
create or write?*

What did you do to encourage my creativity?

What careers did you see in my future?

Was there a time when I expressed
wisdom or maturity beyond my years?

Out of the
Mouths of Babes
Oh, the Things I Said

Do you remember my first words?

What are some funny things I said?

Tell about a time when I said a very bad word, and how you handled it.

What did I say that embarrassed you in public?

Tell Me One More Story *about the things I used to say.*

Chip Off the Old Block

Was It Nature or Nurture?

As a child, I was just like you when I...

As a child, I was just like my dad when I...

<u>Now</u> I'm like you when I...

And I'm like my dad when I...

Tell Me One More Story about how I'm like other members of the family.

I'll Be Back Before You Know It!
Day Care and Babysitters

Who was the best? Why?

Who was the worst? Why?

What did I do when you left me?

Did it ever break your heart to leave me?

Tell Me One More Story *about my time spent with a babysitter.*

This Hurts Me More
Than it Hurts You
Discipline

I must have been naughty once or twice.
Tell me about the things I did when
I was little.

How did you first discipline me?

How about when I got a little older?

111

Did my naughty behavior ever embarrass you in public?

*Was there a time when you let me learn
my lesson the hard way?*

Did the discipline you received as a child affect the way you disciplined me?

What do you feel were the most effective and least effective discipline methods you used on me?

Tell Me One More Story *about the rules at our house.*

Friends
Real and Imaginary

Who were my first playmates, and what did we do?

Other early friends were...

Did I have any imaginary friends?

What do you remember about my first sleepovers away from home?

Do you have a special memory of a sleepover at our house?

Tell about a friend whom you felt was a good influence on me.

Was there a friend who was <u>not</u> a good influence, and what did you do about it?

Was there ever a situation when you wanted to intervene, but chose to let me handle it independently?

Tell Me One More Story *or fond*
memory you have of my friends and me.

126

Just Look at This Pig Sty!
My Room

What did my room look like when I was a baby?

And when I was older?

129

How did I manage my belongings in my room?

What were the first household chores I had, and how did you get me to do them?

Tell Me One More Story *about when I was a big help to you.*

Over the River and Through the Woods
Grandmas and Grandpas

When I was a baby, what did my grandmas and grandpas like to do with me?

134

When I was older, what did I like to do with them?

What did I look forward to most on the way to Grandma and Grandpa's house?

What special things did I learn from my grandparents?

Tell Me One More Story about my grandmas and grandpas.

Mom Always Liked You Best

Sisters and Brothers

When we were little, what did we play?

140

When were we best friends?

What did we fight about?

142

What was your most effective way of handling our squabbling?

In what ways were (are) we most alike?

*In what ways were (are) we
most different?*

Tell Me One More Story about my times
with my sisters or brothers.

How Much is the Doggie in the Window?
Our Pets

*What pets have lived at our house,
and how did I play with them?*

Do you think pets are important in a child's life?
Why or why not?

Tell Me One More Story *about our pets and me.*

Things That Go Bump In the Night
The Monsters Under My Bed

When I was little, what were my fears?

As I got older, what were my worries?

What were <u>your</u> fears and worries concerning me?

Through the years, what have you done to calm my fears?

Tell Me One More Story *about a time when I was frightened.*

My Favorites

Things That Made Me Smile

When I was little, what were my very favorite...

books?

songs?

tv shows?

movies?

clothes?

places to hide?

Through the Year
Memories of
Every Season

Tell me about autumn traditions and holidays we observed.

What autumn sights, scents, tastes and sounds are most nostalgic for you?

__Tell Me One More Story__ about things we did in the fall.

What activities did I like to do in the winter?

What winter traditions and holidays did we observe, and how did we observe them?

What are your most cherished memories of these special days?

Tell Me One More Story about winter.

Tell me about spring holidays and traditions we observed.

We could hardly wait until spring came so we could...

171

What springtime sights, scents, tastes and sounds are most nostalgic for you?

Tell Me One More Story *about springtime.*

What summer traditions and activities did we have?

What do you remember most about those times?

Tell Me One More Story *about a special summer memory.*

Happy Birthday to Me!

My Birthdays

How did we celebrate my first birthday?

What were some other memorable...

traditions?

cakes?

parties?

gifts?

Now that we've outgrown many of those traditions and I'm not always with you on my birthday, how do you observe that special day?

Which birthday of <u>yours</u>, celebrated with me around, stands out in your memory?

Tell about a gift I gave you that meant a lot.

Tell Me One More Story about birthdays at our house.

What Did You Learn Today?
School Days

My first school experience was when I was _____ *years old. I went to...*

_____

_____

_____

What was my reaction to it?

What was it like for you?

What do you remember about my early teachers?

What's the nicest thing a teacher ever told you about me?

What did I have trouble with in school?

189

*Tell me about a day when I came home
from school really happy.*

Tell me about a day when I was really unhappy.

Tell Me One More Story about
school days.

192

Foundations
My Spiritual Upbringing

I was baptized/dedicated at _____

_____

_____

on _____

_____

_____

_____

with _____

_____

_____ *officiating and*

_____

_____

_____

_____ *as godparents/sponsors.*

What are your special memories of that day?

As a child, most of my religious training was at...

Use these pages to tell about important teachers, mentors and milestones in my spiritual upbringing.

How has God answered your most specific prayers for me?

The Way We Were
Styles, Fads and Current Events

What clothing styles were popular when I was a baby?

What popular songs do you remember from that time?

Did you ever have time to watch TV or movies?

What were your favorites?

What inventions do we have around our homes now that weren't widely available when I was a baby?

Who was President of the United States, and what was happening in the news when I was born?

What kinds of cars did our family have in my early years?

Tell me about the houses in which we lived and their addresses.

What changes have you seen in our culture since I was a baby?

Tell Me One More Story *about how things have changed since then.*

208

Looking Back On it All...

*What have been your greatest joys as
a parent?*

Any regrets?

How did you learn to be a parent?

Describe your relationship with your father when you were growing up and living at home. What kinds of things did you and he like to do together?

Describe your relationship with your mother when you were growing up and living at home. What kinds of things did you and she like to do together?

*How did these relationships change
when you left home? As an adult, what
have you most enjoyed doing with your
mom or dad?*

What characteristics of your parents have you noticed in how you parented me?

In what ways was I easy to raise?

In what ways was I difficult to raise?

How do you feel you have been most successful in imparting family values and beliefs?

Do you have a plan for sharing special family treasures with your children and grandchildren after you are gone?

What special holiday or family traditions would you hope will be continued?

What other jobs did you hold while raising me?

Were you ever able to find time for yourself during those years?

If so, what did you like to do?

How did your relationship with my dad change after you had children?

How has your relationship changed since I left home?

What did you do to foster my feelings of self-worth?

How did you teach me about winning and losing?

Tell about how you arrived at the curfews you set for me.

Share your philosophy on giving allowance.

What kind of activities do you feel
helped develop responsibility in me?

*How did you encourage me to do my best
in classwork at school?*

*How did we arrive at the extracurricular
activities I would be involved in from an
early age?*

What age was I when you initiated talks about sexual awareness and how did you do it? Do you recall any of my reactions or questions?

What is your philosophy about the relationship of grandparents and grandchildren?

What would you most like to do for your grandchildren?

Do you have any good advice on how to keep lines of communication open between parent and child?

How did you keep me well and safe while encouraging growth and independence? Do any stories come to mind?

Share your experience and feelings the first time I left home, the bad and the good.

As you think about what interests me today, or what I excel at, can you trace it back to early roots in my childhood?

Tell about a time when you enjoyed watching me gain confidence in something.

Is there anything more you wish you had taught me?

What do you see as my greatest strengths? What do you admire about me?

How have I surprised you?

What have I done that makes you...

happy?

sad?

proud?

worry?

laugh?

cry?

What are your foremost hopes, dreams, wishes, prayers for me?

What advice do you have for me as I…
find a life partner

parent a baby

parent a growing child

parent a teenager

grow older

choose a job

Use these 3 pages to share some special family recipes we have enjoyed through the years.

Share some special family recipes…

248

Tell Me One More Story . . .

Tell Me One More Story . . .

Tell Me One More Story . . .

Tell Me One More Story . . .

Tell Me One More Story . . .

Family Medical History

Because having a family medical history available can be an important tool in diagnosing or preventing many illnesses, these pages have been provided as a point for gathering that information.

Pages have been provided for you to make notes of any occurrences of the conditions listed on the next page. It may also be helpful to record causes and places of family deaths, including possible location of medical records.

Conditions Which May Have Genetic Connections

Cancer

Diabetes

Heart disease, including
   atherosclerosis
   high cholesterol
   high blood pressure

Mental/behavioral conditions, including
   bipolar disorder
   anxiety disorder
   ADHD
   eating disorder
   schizophrenia
   alcoholism

Neurological diseases, including
   Alzheimer's Disease
   ALS (Lou Gehrig's disease
   Tourette Syndrome
   Huntington's Syndrome
   MS
   Tay-Sachs Disease
   Gaucher Disease

Other – allergies, cleft lip or palate, migraine headaches, periodontal disease, arthritis, thalassemia, Hurler's Syndrome, Marfan Syndrome, PKU, clubfoot, cystic fibrosis, hemophilia, obesity, sickle cell anemia, cystic fibrosis

260

Family Medical History

Family Medical History

Family Medical History

Family Medical History